THE ULTIMATE TO DO LIST

—— when ——

YOUR LOVED ONE DIES

BEFORE & AFTER THE FUNERAL

DONNA VINCENT ROA

Limit of Liability/Disclaimer of Warranty: The author and publisher make no representations or warranties with respect to the accuracy and completeness of this book. To do lists like this may not be suitable for every situation. You are urged to consult legal and financial professionals licensed to practice within your state. Neither the publisher nor the author shall be liable for any damages as a result of the actions recommended in this book or websites it references. Because of the dynamic nature of the Internet, any web addresses or links contained in this book may have changed since publication and may no longer be valid. We will make every effort to update these addresses in subsequent versions of the book if changes are needed. For ease of use, web addresses have been shortened using www.bitly.com

Printed in the United States of America

Publisher's Cataloging-in-Publication

Roa, Donna Vincent

The Ultimate To Do List When Your Loved One Dies:
Before & After the Funeral
2012 © Donna Vincent Roa
ISBN-13: 978-0615574844

1. Funeral rites and ceremonies—United States—Planning. 2. Death— Social Aspects. 3. Death— Psychological Aspects. 4. Bereavement. 5. Funeral To Do List

Cover design: Kristie Langone
Author photo: Jeremy Chichister-Miles
Inside design: TM Design, Inc.
Editor: Beth Goodrich

To my mother, best friend and life coach.
May she rest in eternal peace.

MARGIE BROUSSARD VINCENT
November 7, 1929 – January 12, 2011

TABLE of CONTENTS

FOREWORD

It's 2 a.m., and the phone rings. You either hesitate answering the phone, or you race to get it knowing that a call at that hour is never good news. If a loved one has died and you are responsible for handling the funeral arrangements, the next 48 to 72 hours are going to be a mad rush for you and your family, especially if you aren't prepared.

The shock of the death, in addition to the sheer number of urgent decisions and details associated with funeral planning, is overwhelming for even the most organized person. The ordeal tests your sense of planning, as well as your memory, patience, finances and relationships.

The dreaded feeling of "What did I forget to do?" weighs heavy on you as you struggle to take care of the multitude of unfamiliar tasks that need to be accomplished. The practical and emotional challenges associated with what needs to be done before, during and after the funeral service leave you no time to grieve.

This scenario and these feelings that I describe are real to me. We all know that death is inevitable, but how many of us really think about it, talk about it, or adequately prepare for it?

My loving mother passed away on January 12, 2011, and I and my two sisters, Julie Matte and Karen Perron, were responsible for carrying out her wishes, planning her funeral, and taking care of everything else that followed. None of us had served in this role before.

In the few hours I had to prepare for my trip from Maryland to Louisiana, I searched for a comprehensive to do list similar to this book, but none existed. I didn't have time to read 250 pages about end-of-life decisions. I needed a process map to guide what would happen next. I had never "done" a funeral before.

I took some comfort in knowing that we had met with a lawyer a few years back to set up my mother and father's last will and testament, advanced directives/living will, power of attorney, and other legal documents. I knew also that she had purchased burial plots and had a small insurance policy to cover her funeral. That was about it.

Like most families, regrettably, we never took the time to discuss the specific end-of-life details and funeral arrangements. I wish we had done so.

And because we had not talked to her about these things prior to her passing, during this process, we continually asked ourselves, "What would Mama want?" for all the decisions we faced. The only thing we could recall concretely was that she wanted to be buried in a pine box. We did our best.

The Ultimate To Do List When Your Loved One Dies: Before & After the Funeral will help keep you organized, reduce your stress and burden, and help you to approach these necessary tasks with calm and confidence.

Reviewing what needs to be accomplished and making many of these decisions prior to death will ensure that your loved one's beliefs, personal philosophy, preferences, and budget are addressed while they still can be.

A large majority of the tasks enumerated in this book can be discussed, decided upon, and completed prior to someone's death. Through a concerted effort at pro-active funeral planning, you or someone responsible for taking care of your funeral will have the information needed to carry out final arrangements and wishes with ease and confidence when death happens.

If you are completing this book for yourself in preparation for death, please make sure to keep this book and other details of your funeral plan and estate in a safe place. Advise your executor or next of kin of where you have placed this and other important life documents.

My wish is that every person and household has a copy of this simple to-do list, action plan and resource list. Discussing the details you provide in this book and other estate planning efforts will ensure that others understand your wants, wishes and intentions. They will be able to carry out what you envision happening before and after your death. Use this book to help express your thoughts.

This book was created as a guide for you to use in planning your funeral or that of someone you love. Because of the ever-changing laws and their interpretation, it is recommended that, where necessary, you discuss these matters with appropriate advisors and professionals.

In most situations, it is wise to contact an attorney for estate planning and to assist you with putting together a will, a living will or medical directive, power of attorney, and other legal documents. An attorney can advise you of the actions you need to take that are applicable to your unique circumstances.

For complicated financial situations and where large estates or businesses are involved, you should also consult an accountant. Pro-active legal and financial counseling will help you to avoid lawsuits and further complications in settling an estate.

While I've tried to make *The Ultimate To Do List When Your Loved One Dies* as comprehensive as possible to ensure that you know the kinds of things that need to be accomplished, not all items may be applicable to your situation. Every funeral is influenced by religious and cultural traditions, personal preferences, philosophy, and cost.

~~~

Even though we exist in a death-averse society and typically avoid conversations about death, we shouldn't allow this to affect our preparedness or prevent us from putting a plan in place.

Death comes to each of us and is a natural part of life. I believe this book will help us to be ready for death and to systematize what we need to do prior to death.

Life planning conversations and taking an active role in your or a family member's funeral arrangements can transform a painful and stressful occasion into one of great meaning and peace for all of those involved. This book will help you to be prepared.

I realize now I wasn't prepared for my Mother's funeral. And because of this, I missed the chance to properly grieve during her funeral and Mass because I was so caught up in ensuring that everything was in place. The small notebook I carried with me to document what I needed to do held so much value for me. That small notebook became this book.

My Mother's life and passing inspired me to create this book and pass value to others. I have written it in honor of her sweet and loving memory. She would be proud.

God bless you and your family. Just remember...love never dies.

Donna Vincent Roa
donna@funeraltodolist.com

NEAR *and* UPON DEATH

1. *First Steps*

☐ If death occurs in a hospital or hospice, confer with the medical personnel about the procedures that take place following death.

☐ Locate the decedent's living will.

☐ Share the living will with medical authorities.

☐ Notify authorities of the death. Who you notify will depend on the circumstances of the death (e.g., police, coroner, etc.). An autopsy may be necessary.

☐ If the death was unanticipated, call 911.

☐ Call the coroner. Corner contact information:

_____

_____

_____

☐ Arrange for the administration of last rites.

☐ Officiate contact information:

_____

_____

_____

☐ Spend time with your loved one to say your good-byes and honor the grieving process.

☐ Meet with family members to discuss your loved one's wishes, funeral arrangements, and administrative and financial decisions surrounding the funeral.

☐ If appropriate for your situation, ask a clergy member to assist you with the funeral and burial arrangements.

_____

_____

_____

☐ Set and share your goals for the service.

    ☐ Goal #1:

    _____

    _____

    _____

    ☐ Goal #2:

    _____

    _____

    _____

    ☐ Goal #3:

    _____

    _____

    _____

☐ Visualize the kind of service that you want.

☐ Determine the team of family members or friends who will be involved in helping you with the funeral arrangements. Record their names and contact information here.

_____

_____

_____

_____

_____

☐ Determine lines of responsibility and who will do what tasks.

☐ Discuss non-traditional funeral and options.
   ☐ Conservation burial
   ☐ Funeral at home
   ☐ Home burial
   ☐ Cremation
   ☐ Tribute ceremony in a nursing facility
   ☐ Shroud
   ☐ Locally made caskets
   ☐ Carbon-neutral caskets
   ☐ Burial at sea

☐ Obtain state rules and regulations applicable to home burials. Your state may require some assistance from a funeral home in the handling of your loved one's body.

☐ Ask assistance from home burial organizations, your pastor or priest, or a death mid-wife.

☐ If death occurs in a state other than the decedent's place of residence, call a funeral home in the target state (it is more cost-effective this way) to begin preparations, handle the transfer, and file the necessary paperwork to secure the official transfer.

☐ You may want to ask questions about how a body is prepared for delivery to the funeral home.

☐ Confirm arrangements for transferring the body from place of death to funeral home.

☐ Provide name and contact information of the funeral home to the team preparing the body for transfer.

☐ Determine if loved one wanted to donate his or her organs or body parts (e.g., notation on driver's license or in will or other legal document).

☐ Locate will and other estate papers and record where they are kept.

_____

_____

_____

☐ If no will exists, you may want to contact your county or parish probate court and an attorney for legal advice, especially for larger estates.

☐ Locate pre-paid burial plan or contract.

☐ Gather other important papers.
  ☐ Birth certificate
  ☐ Marriage certificate(s)
  ☐ Social Security number/card
  ☐ Insurance policies
  ☐ Tax returns
  ☐ Bills
  ☐ Loan payment books
  ☐ Deeds (including that for the cemetery plot/grave)
  ☐ Military discharge papers
  ☐ Vehicle registrations
  ☐ Earning statements
  ☐ Bank account documentation
  ☐ Union payment information
  ☐ Annuities
  ☐ Pre-nuptial agreements
  ☐ Divorce papers
  ☐ Budgets
  ☐ Bookkeeping records
  ☐ Check registers
  ☐ Bank statements
  ☐ Bankruptcy papers
  ☐ Existence of trust
  ☐ Pension retirement benefits
  ☐ Business agreements
  ☐ Documentation of business ownership or interest
  ☐ Documentation of the value of personal property

  ☐ _____

  ☐ _____

  ☐ _____

  ☐ _____

  ☐ _____

- ☐ Need to replace vital documents and other personal records? Visit USA.gov, the U.S. Government's official web portal. Replace your vital documents.
  - ☐ http://1.usa.gov/rN2gbl

- ☐ Locate keys.
  - ☐ House(s)
  - ☐ Car(s)
  - ☐ Safety deposit box
  - ☐ Boat
  - ☐ _____
  - ☐ _____
  - ☐ _____

- ☐ Determine membership in a burial or memorial society.

- ☐ Look for instructions or documents that the decedent may have prepared detailing funeral and burial arrangements.

- ☐ If decedent was a child under 18, hire an attorney to represent him or her.

- ☐ Identify executor of the estate:

_____

_____

_____

☐ Contact your local Department of Social Services before contracting funeral arrangements. Burial assistance may be available if the decedent was receiving public assistance.

_____

_____

_____

_____

_____

_____

_____

_____

_____

_____

2. Identify Final Resting Place and Funeral Home

☐ Determine if you want environmentally sustainable death care practices applied to your situation.
   ☐ The Green Burial Council
      • 888-966-3330
      • http://bit.ly/s9wWiF
   ☐ Funeral Consumers Alliance
      • 802-865-8300
      • http://www.funerals.org/

- ☐ Shop around for the right funeral home to get the best services and value for your money (e.g., Google your location and the word "funeral home," look in the Yellow Pages, or ask for friend/family recommendations).

- ☐ Visit the website of several local funeral homes. Evaluate their service offerings and determine their ability to provide comfort and support in your time of need.

- ☐ Get price quotes over the phone to determine which facility/facilities you will visit.

- ☐ For in-person visits, obtain an itemized price list of services, and view the facilities and caskets.

- ☐ Explore casket purchases from other retailers.
  - ☐ Costco
  - ☐ Walmart
  - ☐ Best Price Caskets
    - 866-474-5061
    - http://bit.ly/sSiL9Y
  - ☐ 24Hour Caskets
    - 888-817-3001
    - http://bit.ly/sKMymG
  - ☐ Southern Craft Manufacturing
    - 800-413-1778
    - http://bit.ly/southerncraft
  - ☐ Trappist Caskets
    - 888-433-6934
    - http://bit.ly/trappistcaskets
  - ☐ Abbey Caskets
    - 800-987-7380
    - http://bit.ly/abbeycaskets
  - ☐ Final Footprint – Green Caskets
    - 650-726-5255
    - http://bit.ly/finalfootprint

☐ Compare prices and services before you make a final decision.

☐ Funeral home location and contact information:

_____

_____

_____

_____

_____

☐ Obtain or prepare a map to the funeral home for visitors and guests.

☐ Gather information for completion of death certificate.

☐ Locate deed to cemetery plot/grave.

☐ If none exists, visit selected cemetery or memorial gardens and purchase right of interment (grave) opening/closing, and vault or mausoleum. A columbarium, which is a miniature version of a mausoleum, can also be purchased for urn placement. Perpetual care fees for the cemetery maintenance fund are also typically included in the sale.

☐ Obtain/identify/visit vault.

☐ Obtain/identify/visit mausoleum.

☐ If interment will be in a columbarium or mausoleum, you may want to purchase a small plaque for placement outside the burial chamber. This may be done after burial.

☐ Get a copy of the cemetery's rules and regulations, including ones that address grave decorations and size and type restrictions for the mausoleum plaque marker.

☐ Cemetery and plot/grave location and vendor contact information:

_____

_____

_____

_____

_____

☐ Purchase grave marker.
Grave marker budget: _____

☐ Decide what you want written on the grave marker.

_____

_____

_____

_____

_____

☐ Order grave marker engraving.
  ☐ Veteran's plaque
  ☐ Special insignia
  ☐ Fraternal organization seal
  ☐ Other _____

□ Purchase memorial garden bench or other memorial item for cemetery.

□ Set up date and time with funeral director to meet and discuss funeral arrangements.

_____

_____

_____

_____

_____

_____

FUNERAL ARRANGEMENTS

1. *Prepare to Meet the Funeral Director*

- ☐ Place of wake or funeral service:
  - ☐ Family home
  - ☐ Church
  - ☐ Funeral home
  - ☐ Graveside ceremony (committal service)
  - ☐ Other _____

- ☐ Place of memorial service:
  - ☐ Family home
  - ☐ Church
  - ☐ Funeral home
  - ☐ Graveside ceremony (committal service)
  - ☐ Other _____

- ☐ Decide and arrange the date and time of the wake/visitation and funeral service.

  _____

  _____

  _____

- ☐ Select deceased's burial dress items, including clothing, undergarments, shoes and jewelry.

  _____

  _____

  _____

☐ Determine items to place on decedent or in the casket (e.g., eyeglasses, rosary, playing cards, baseball, guitar pick, gardening glove, cell phone, mementos, photos, something that the deceased would deem special, important, necessary, etc.).

_____

_____

_____

_____

☐ Notify funeral director if you'd like to have final jewelry returned to a specific family member.

☐ Determine casket or urn budget before you arrive at funeral home.
   $ _____

☐ Contact personal hairdresser to arrange hair styling or discuss other arrangements with the funeral director.

☐ Decide if you want to have photos or video taken at home and/or during the service.
   ☐ Photos
   ☐ Videos

☐ Hire photographer or videographer.

_____

_____

_____

- ☐ Request information, pricing, and availability from the funeral director about funeral and memorial live and delayed webcasting to enable family and friends who are unable to attend the service to view it over the Internet in the privacy of their home.

- ☐ Deliver clothing, jewelry and other items to the funeral home.

- ☐ Create a personalized life tribute book for your loved one.
    - ☐ http://bit.ly/tPRwQM

2. At the Funeral Home: Choose and Order Necessary Items

- ☐ Present life insurance papers to the funeral director.
- ☐ Present cemetery plot deed to the funeral director.
- ☐ Choose casket type.
    - ☐ Wood
    - ☐ Metal
    - ☐ Wicker
    - ☐ Bamboo
    - ☐ Paper
    - ☐ Other _____

- ☐ View casket selection in funeral home.

- ☐ Decide whether to have an open or closed casket for the wake and funeral service.

- ☐ Will the body be cremated?

- ☐ If cremation, choose the urn.
    - ☐ Cremation Urns for Ashes
        - http://bit.ly/cremationurns
    - ☐ Mainly Urns
        - http://bit.ly/ug2k18
    - ☐ Urnseller.com – Quality Cremation Urns
        - http://bit.ly/qualityurns
    - ☐ Biodegradable Urns
        - http://bit.ly/biodegradableurns
    - ☐ Urns Approved for Travel
        - http://bit.ly/tIyuSU
        - http://bit.ly/seEf79
        - http://bit.ly/uBic26

- ☐ Scatter ashes.
    - ☐ Location: _____

- ☐ Rent a casket from the funeral service provider if body is presented before cremation.

- ☐ Order memorial cards.

- ☐ Order laminated scripture bookmarks.

- ☐ Present special needs to funeral director.

_____

_____

_____

_____

- ☐ Confirm with the funeral director use of visitation rooms for private family meetings.

☐ Confirm access to kitchen or eating area of the funeral home.

☐ Confirm if the funeral home will or can provide food and beverages.

☐ Confirm that condolences can be put on the funeral home website.

☐ Confirm and provide the mailing address for the person who should receive the final summary of the condolences that are put on the website.

☐ Confirm that funeral home will coordinate memorial service with church, synagogue, or at another venue.

☐ Confirm that funeral home will coordinate activities with burial site service provider. Provide name and contact information.

☐ Confirm eulogy with funeral director.

    ☐ Time and date: _____

    ☐ Speaker: _____

    ☐ Length: _____

☐ Determine if you want an "open mike" for well-wishers to speak at the wake or funeral service.

☐ Announce to funeral goers that in place of a eulogy, you will have people share brief stories or thoughts on a microphone that will be passed around the room or people may go to the podium.

    ☐ Suggest a time limit

☐ Discuss make-up preferences with funeral director.

☐ Discuss flower preferences: lid arrangement/floral piece for inside the casket, a standing spray, or something else.

_____

_____

_____

_____

_____

☐ Ask the funeral director to recommend a florist nearby the funeral home.

☐ Order death certificates from funeral home. You may need up to 10, depending on the complexity of the estate. Photocopies are generally not accepted for the follow-up transactions.
  ☐ Social Security
  ☐ Closing credit card and bank accounts
  ☐ Insurance companies
  ☐ Family members
  ☐ For access to safety deposit boxes

☐ Choose funeral home wake/visitation music preferences.

_____

_____

_____

☐ Prepare set of photos for a keepsake CD (can be prepared by you or by the funeral home for a fee).
  ☐ Baby
  ☐ School years
  ☐ Graduation
  ☐ Marriage
  ☐ Children
  ☐ Weddings
  ☐ Grandchildren
  ☐ Special events
  ☐ Other _____

☐ Choose background music for the story CD (e.g., favorite songs, meaningful songs, wedding dance song, original songs, etc.).

_____

_____

_____

☐ Provide pictures and music selection to funeral director for story CD to display during visitation.

☐ Order extra photo CDs from funeral home to distribute to friends and family.

☐ Order and set up memory or guest book.

☐ Confirm with funeral director if you would like to display personal photos in photo frames.

☐ Gather photos and reframe special photos, if necessary.

☐ Confirm collection and removal of personal photo display after the funeral.

- [ ] Set up a memory table.
  - [ ] Awards
  - [ ] Plaques for work achievement
  - [ ] Military insignias and medals
  - [ ] Special trinkets
  - [ ] Musical instruments
  - [ ] Uniforms
  - [ ] Personal collections

- [ ] Decide if you would like charitable donations in lieu of flowers and notify the funeral director.

- [ ] Choose charity to list in death announcement:

  _____

  _____

  _____

  _____

- [ ] Decide if you would like any other forms of symbolism or rituals.

  _____

  _____

  _____

  _____

- [ ] Advise funeral director if/when/where a reception will be held in the event people ask if they could bring food donations.

☐ Confirm with funeral director website submission capability for condolences.

☐ Provide funeral home with mailing address of recipient of those condolences.

3. Obituary

☐ Confirm with the funeral director the cost of running the obituaries (i.e., newspaper, on-line, television).

☐ Locate the latest resume of the deceased. This will help with the obituary and the eulogy.

☐ Compose obituary, or if an obituary was previously prepared, retrieve and update as necessary.

☐ Have a second person review the draft obituary for errors before publication.

☐ Determine obituary publication date(s).

_____

_____

_____

_____

☐ Confirm which papers will publish the obituary.

_____

_____

_____

_____

_____

☐ Confirm which television stations will publish the obituary. Some community stations offer this service.

☐ Self-publish the obituary or a short announcement on Facebook, member association page, in an email to colleagues, etc.

☐ Self-publish the obituary on www.tributes.com, an online resource for local and national obituary news. At the time of publishing this book, the site charges a one-time payment of $299 for the Eternal Tribute. A Photo Obituary and Military Tribute are also available for a fee.

4. Arrange Funeral Seating and Transportation

☐ Discuss seating arrangements for funeral service, if any.

☐ Arrange transportation for funeral coach, family limo, clergy car, pallbearers, and flower car.

☐ Special transportation requests:

_____

_____

_____

_____

_____

☐ Transportation for immediate family to grave site:

_____

_____

_____

_____

☐ Order of cars to gravesite:

_____

_____

_____

_____

☐ Confirm pallbearers and contact information:

_____

_____

_____

_____

_____

☐ Confirm that funeral home will generate thank-you notes for the pallbearers. If not...

☐ Write thank you notes to pallbearers.

5. Final Steps: Confirm and Coordinate

☐ Create a program for the service.

☐ Choose type of eulogy.
   ☐ Presentational eulogy
   ☐ Video eulogy

☐ Decide who will deliver the eulogy and speak with him or her about the requirements, the scheduled time, and what is expected.

_____

_____

_____

☐ Gather information for the eulogy.

☐ Write the eulogy. Capture the character of the deceased. Prepare a celebration of life message. Talk about precious memories. Information to include:

_____

_____

_____

_____

_____

_____

_____

_____

☐ Prepare thank you card and envelope for officiant honorarium (e.g., a typical donation is $100. If you choose, more can be given).

☐ Give honorarium to officiant.

☐ Visit cemetery management office to present plot papers and inform manager of loved one's death.

☐ Visit and confirm plot location.

☐ Confirm dress code and communicate with guests if it is non-traditional.

☐ Confirm that there are no program or agenda changes.

☐ Confirm delivery of flowers by funeral home.
  ☐ Your residence
  ☐ Donate to:
    • Church
    • Nursing homes
    • Assisted living
    • Friends
    • Family

Date: _____

Time: _____

Location: _____

_____

_____

☐ Make sure the guestbook is placed near the entrance where service will take place.

☐ Set up table with photos and special items for display.

☐ Set aside time to talk to family members about ways to handle potentially awkward situations, and pre-identify an interventionist for diffusing them.

☐ Decide what you, your children, and family will wear to the funeral.

☐ Take a moment to thank your funeral-planning team for their help.

MILITARY FUNERAL

- ☐ Branch of service: _____

- ☐ Determine eligibility for military funeral honors.
  - ☐ http://1.usa.gov/uAb5Rc

- ☐ Notify the Veterans Benefits Administration of the death of a veteran or benefit recipient.

- ☐ If you have questions or need to request information on burial and mortuary benefits, learn about the benefits available to surviving family members and how to make these arrangements, call the Veteran Benefits Administration.
  - ☐ 800-827-1000

- ☐ Military funerals must be provided (by law) if requested by the family of an eligible deceased veteran. This includes honor guard details, flag folding, and playing of Taps by a bugler or by recording if a bugler is not available.
  - ☐ http://1.usa.gov/ugX8A7

- ☐ Make sure you have a copy of the DD-214 Form – Proof of Military Service. If you cannot locate the form, military personnel records can be obtained for no cost with the form SF-180 at:
  - ☐ http://1.usa.gov/vR9ZNV

- ☐ Explore Department of Veterans Affairs no-cost bereavement counseling services for veteran family members.
  - ☐ 202-461-6530
  - ☐ vetcenter.bereavement@va.gov

☐ Visit the US Department of Veteran Affairs, Office of Survivors Assistance website to get more information.
  ☐ http://1.usa.gov/w1cV2G
  ☐ officeofsurvivors@va.gov

☐ Order a Government-provided headstone or marker through the funeral director, cemetery official, or VA counselor.
  ☐ Fill out VA Form 40-1330
  ☐ http://1.usa.gov/vfm5ir

☐ Obtain a burial flag from the VA. Apply for the flag by completing VA Form 21-2008, Application for United States Flag for Burial Purposes.
  ☐ 800-827-1000
  ☐ http://1.usa.gov/burialflag

☐ Visit military cemetery website for additional burial information, including burial benefits, burial allowance benefits, and burial in a private cemetery or burial at sea.
  ☐ http://1.usa.gov/vesStD

☐ Order a Presidential Memorial Certificate to honor the memory of your loved one. Multiple copies, which are signed by the current President, can be ordered with VA Form 40-0247.
  ☐ http://1.usa.gov/vuM1YK

☐ Check eligibility for burial in a national cemetery burial.
  ☐ http://1.usa.gov/ts4pig

☐ To schedule a burial, call the National Cemetery Scheduling Office.
  ☐ 866-900-6417

- ☐ For follow up questions or issues about a National Cemetery burial, contact Veterans Affairs.
  - ☐ 800-535-1117
  - ☐ http://www.cem.va.gov/

- ☐ Visit Arlington National Cemetery website for information on a burial there.
  - ☐ http://www.bit.ly/rA1NwE

- ☐ If burial is to take place in a national cemetery, discharge papers should be submitted to the funeral home director, who can assist you with making burial arrangements.

- ☐ Purchase flag box or medallion display case.

- ☐ Engage Eternal Reefs military honors program and ask for a military discount.
  - ☐ 888-423-7333
  - ☐ http://bit.ly/eternalreefs
  - ☐ info@eternalreefs.com
  - ☐ Provider Directory: http://bit.ly/rxbVp9

- ☐ Obtain details about navy burials.
  - ☐ U.S. Navy Mortuary Affairs Office
    Casualty Assistance Branch
    Naval Personnel Command (NPC-621)
    5720 Integrity Drive
    Millington, TN 38055-6210
  - ☐ 800-368-3202
  - ☐ http://1.usa.gov/vZeaHJ

FLOWERS

☐ Determine budget for flowers.

$ _____

☐ Choose a florist.

Name: _____

Address: _____

_____

_____

Phone: _____

☐ Share with the florist details about the deceased's life, hobbies, personality, occupation, interests, etc.

☐ Consult with the florist regarding any specifications, restrictions, or regulations of the funeral site.

☐ Provide florist and funeral director with each other's phone numbers.

☐ Check cemetery requirements prior to graveside flowers purchase.

☐ Purchase arrangement that can be laid at the graveside.

☐ Determine preference in flowers, colors, and types of arrangements.

☐ Determine flower arrangements for the outside of the casket presentation.
  ☐ Full length casket spray for closed casket
  ☐ Half-length casket spray for open casket
  ☐ Standing spray
  ☐ Cross
  ☐ Wreath
  ☐ Heart
  ☐ Plants
  ☐ Baskets
  ☐ Vase arrangement
  ☐ Display table arrangement
  ☐ Live plant
  ☐ Other _____
  ☐ For military funerals where a flag is draped on the casket, only standing flower sprays are used for the service.

☐ Determine lid arrangement or floral pieces for inside the casket presentation.
  ☐ Wrist bouquet
  ☐ Corsage
  ☐ Boutonniere
  ☐ Other _____

☐ Order and purchase boutonnieres for pallbearers.
  ☐ Number needed: _____

☐ Determine if any special trinkets or items are to be put on the casket flower arrangement or standing flower arrangements (e.g., crosses, hearts, playing cards, or other personal items).

☐ Deliver special trinkets to florist for insertion into flower arrangement.

☐ Ask the florist to provide a summary list of the names and addresses of those who gave flowers and a brief description of the type of arrangement or plant that was given. This will be especially helpful for writing the thank-you notes.

☐ In the case of a tragic death, flowers (e.g., garlands, bouquets, wreaths or single stems) may be placed on or near the site where the death occurred.

MEMORIAL SERVICE *or* MASS ARRANGEMENTS

☐ Type of service: _____

☐ Officiant: _____

☐ Flowers: _____

☐ Music selections for the service:

_____

_____

_____

_____

_____

_____

_____

_____

_____

☐ If hymns will be sung, verify that those you select are in the hymnals at the location of the service.

☐ Determine budget for hiring musicians. $_____

☐ Choose organist or arrange for church to provide one:

_____

_____

☐ Singers or other musicians:

_____

_____

_____

_____

_____

_____

_____

☐ Special readings (text or poems):

_____

_____

_____

_____

_____

_____

_____

☐ Ceremony participants:

_____

_____

_____

_____

_____

_____

☐ Determine if there will be a special gathering after the memorial services.

Budget: _____

Date: _____

Place: _____

Time: _____

Caterer? (if any): _____

_____

Food: _____

_____

_____

Special dietary considerations: _____

_____

_____

_____

Prep/clean up: _____

_____

_____

_____

☐ Determine food/catering needs prior to or during the wake and/or funeral.

_____

_____

_____

_____

_____

_____

☐ Determine food needs/catering for after the funeral.

_____

_____

_____

_____

_____

_____

_____

☐ If needed, call local hotels for reservations and special rates for family and friends.

_____

_____

_____

_____

_____

_____

_____

☐ Secure and/or designate alternative accommodations for relatives and out of town guests.

_____

_____

_____

_____

_____

_____

_____

_____

AFTER *the* FUNERAL

1. *Take Time to Honor Your Loved One*

☐ Take time to mourn and celebrate the mark the person made on this world.

☐ Submit Mass or service dedications.

☐ Tribute luncheon or dinner (typically paid for by the family of the deceased).

☐ Location of restaurant:

_____

_____

☐ Donate extra plants from the funeral to recipients chosen in pre-funeral planning stage.

☐ Make commemorative donations to charities, churches, endowments, etc.

☐ Purchase and deliver grave flower arrangement.

☐ Schedule a planting (e.g., tree, shrubs) for a lasting and permanent memorial.

☐ Seek out grief counseling.

☐ Contact support groups or individual counselors at signs of depression.

☐ Make a video or picture collage.

2. Notify Social Security

☐ Locate decedent's social security number.

☐ If surviving spouse is available for the call to Social Security
Administration, have ready:
  ☐ Marriage date/marriage license
  ☐ Place of work
  ☐ Other personal details
  ☐ In addition to this being a notification of death call, this
     will also be a "proof of marriage" conversation.

☐ Notify the Social Security Administration local or national
   office as soon as possible (open 7 a.m. – 7 p.m.) to make
   sure that the family receives all of the benefits to which it
   may be entitled.
  ☐ 800-772-1213
  ☐ http://1.usa.gov/tiCTzB

☐ Mail (certified mail) original death certificate to:
  ☐ Social Security Administration
     P.O. Box 25447
     Attn: Unit 550
     Denver Federal Ctr.
     Denver, CO 80225

☐ Notify surviving spouse (in same household) that Social
   Security Administration will send a one-time, lump-sum
   death payment of $255.

☐ If a Social Security Administration monthly payment is
   received following death of loved one (during the month
   of death or after), you need to return the payment(s) to
   the Social Security Administration. Generally, the SSA will
   automatically withdraw payments made via direct deposit.

- ☐ If the Social Security Administration monthly payment is paid by check, it must be returned.

- ☐ If the Social Security Administration paid by direct deposit, notify bank and request that any direct deposit funds received for the month of death or later be returned to the Social Security Administration.

- ☐ Advise surviving spouse that he or she will receive the larger SSA monthly benefit payments of the two, but will not receive both.
  - ☐ http://1.usa.gov/vtKQ34

3. Tie Up the Loose Ends of the Decedent's Affairs

- ☐ Locate password list.

- ☐ Determine method of access to decedent's personal computer files, if locked.

- ☐ Review checkbooks and credit card statements for additional information or items that need follow-up.

- ☐ Obtain proof of loans made and debts owed.

- ☐ Gather and pay all outstanding bills.

- ☐ Beware of fraudulent invoices, questionable mail solicitations, or phone calls requesting personal information, demanding action on behalf of your loved one, or making claims that lack documentation.

☐ Handle or assign additional outstanding financial
obligations:

_____

_____

_____

_____

_____

_____

_____

_____

_____

_____

☐ Update account information on all joint financial accounts.

☐ If necessary, open a bank account for the decedent's estate
to properly account for the assets and administration
expenses.

☐ Remove decedent's name from all jointly owned assets.

☐ Access decedent's personal calendar and cancel upcoming
appointments.

- ☐ Cancel health insurance.

- ☐ Cancel dental insurance.

- ☐ Notify pharmacy of death.

- ☐ Cancel prescriptions.

- ☐ Modify/cancel car insurance policy.

- ☐ Cancel motor club policies (e.g., AAA, AARP, All State, Geico, etc.).

- ☐ Locate life insurance policies.

- ☐ Call life insurance company and provide date and time of death, information about surviving spouse, burial details, etc.

- ☐ Send original death certificate to life insurance company.

- ☐ File life insurance claim.

- ☐ Notify primary doctor of loved one's passing.

- ☐ Obtain health records from primary doctor.

- ☐ Obtain health records from hospital(s).

☐ Notify credit card companies and remove name from accounts or cancel credit card accounts altogether.

☐ _____

_____

☐ _____

_____

☐ _____

_____

☐ _____

_____

☐ _____

_____

☐ _____

_____

☐ _____

_____

☐ _____

_____

☐ File veteran benefits claim, if applicable.

☐ File union benefits claim, if applicable.

☐ Report death to the Railroad Retirement Board, if applicable.
  ☐ 877-772-5772

☐ Explore/identify professional organizations' death benefit.

☐ Close/cash out retirement accounts.

☐ Close/cash out online brokerage account(s).

☐ Establish a perpetual endowment fund.

☐ Contact broker regarding investments (e.g., IRAs, Roth IRAs, college savings plans, money market accounts, mutual funds, etc.):

☐ _____

_____

☐ _____

_____

☐ _____

_____

☐ _____

_____

☐ _____

_____

☐ _____

_____

☐ _____

_____

☐ Stocks and savings bonds:

    ☐ _____

    _____

    ☐ _____

    _____

    ☐ _____

    _____

    ☐ _____

    _____

    ☐ _____

    _____

    ☐ _____

    _____

    ☐ _____

    _____

☐ Close bank accounts:

    ☐ _____

    _____

    ☐ _____

    _____

    ☐ _____

    _____

☐ _____

_____

☐ _____

_____

☐ _____

_____

☐ Contact shareholder services for direct reinvestment programs (DRIP) to provide notification of death.

☐ Evaluate beneficiary list on DRIP documentation and facilitate disbursement.

☐ Determine and carry out necessary real estate transactions:

_____

_____

_____

_____

_____

_____

_____

☐ Terminate decedent's lease on residential property.

☐ Change titles and deeds to properties:

_____

_____

_____

_____

_____

_____

_____

☐ For right of survivorship property, ownership passes to the survivor.

☐ For out-of-state property ownership and settlement issues, contact an attorney.

☐ Determine if ancillary administrations are needed.

    ☐ Loans: _____

    _____

    _____

    _____

    _____

    _____

    _____

☐ Mortgages: _____

_____

_____

_____

_____

☐ Annuities: _____

_____

_____

_____

☐ Trust funds: _____

_____

_____

_____

_____

☐ Review contents of personal safe.

- ☐ Review contents of decedent's purse or wallet and determine if you need to take action on any item.
    - ☐ Close credit card accounts and cut up cards
    - ☐ Cut up grocery store cards
    - ☐ Safely store check book
    - ☐ Distribute purse contents
    - ☐ Give away personal items

- ☐ Obtain safety deposit box key.

- ☐ Arrange with bank or other institution for safety deposit box opening.

- ☐ Contact an attorney to make arrangements for any ownership of a business.

- ☐ Determine if a buy-sell agreement was put in place (i.e., interests may be purchased by the business or other business owners).

- ☐ Close business owned by the decedent or put under management of capable person.

- ☐ Search for other assets.
    - ☐ Other assets identified:

_____

_____

_____

_____

_____

_____

_____

_____

_____

_____

_____

☐ Meet with accountant to determine projected taxes.

☐ File Federal tax return.

☐ File state tax return.

☐ File state and Federal estate tax return.

☐ Pay taxes out of estate.

☐ Distribute tax refunds according to the will.

☐ For all utilities and monthly services, determine if cancellation is necessary or a name substitution/change is necessary.

☐ Cancel electricity.

☐ Cancel home phone/internet service.

☐ Cancel cable service.

☐ Cancel cell phone service.

☐ Cancel credit cards and let card companies know that the cardholder has died. (Some may require death certificate to cancel.)

☐ Cancel health club membership.

☐ Cancel association or fraternal memberships.

☐ Cancel pest control service or contract.

☐ Cancel magazine subscriptions.

☐ Cancel newspaper subscriptions.

☐ Cancel library card.

☐ Cancel catalogs.

☐ Cancel online monthly services.

☐ Close personal networking accounts and blogs.
    ☐ LinkedIn
      • Address: _____
      • Password: _____
    ☐ Twitter
      • Address: _____
      • Password: _____
    ☐ Flickr
      • Address: _____
      • Password: _____
    ☐ WordPress
      • Address: _____
      • Password: _____
    ☐ Blogger.com site(s)
      • Address: _____
      • Password: _____

☐ Request that Facebook profile be memorialized. Must have proof of death (e.g., online obituary or death listing in newspaper) and Facebook address.
    ☐ http://on.fb.me/ttSRok

- ☐ Or, request that Facebook profile be deleted.
- ☐ Close LinkedIn account by filling in Verification of Death Form.
    - ☐ http://bit.ly/shN8kr

- ☐ Conduct a Google search (www.google.com) using the decedent's name to determine if additional action is required.

- ☐ Shut down known email accounts.
    - ☐ Address: _____
      Password: _____
    - ☐ Address: _____
      Password: _____
    - ☐ Address: _____
      Password: _____

4. Settle Estate

- ☐ If necessary, contact attorney for reading of the will.

- ☐ Contact family members for reading of the will.

- ☐ Contact attorney and update will or create a new one for the surviving spouse.

- ☐ Send death certificate to:

    - ☐ _____
      _____

    - ☐ _____
      _____

    - ☐ _____

☐ _____

☐ _____

☐ _____

☐ _____

☐ _____

☐ If the estate is insolvent (debts exceed value), consult an estate attorney.

☐ Consult an estate attorney before paying any debts.

☐ Consult an attorney if estate administration is required for a blended family (e.g., stepchildren, second spouse).

☐ Consult an attorney for filing tax returns of large estate.

☐ Consult an attorney if decedent's trust is a continuing trust to determine your duties and powers as trustee.

☐ Dismiss collection agencies that try to convince you that you are responsible for payment on a card owned solely by your deceased loved one.

- ☐ Report any problems you have with a debt collector.
  - ☐ Your state Attorney General's office
    - www.naag.org
  - ☐ Federal Trade Commission
    - www.ftc.gov

- ☐ Check for immigration, citizenship papers, or any other outstanding legal process to discuss with attorney.

- ☐ Collect all income, money, and receivables due to descendent.

- ☐ Determine what cash is needed to settle the estate. Make estate distributions.

_____

_____

_____

_____

_____

_____

- ☐ Distribute assets in accordance with the will.

- ☐ Obtain certified copies of the will, if necessary.

5. *Clean Up Living Space and Make Arrangements for Surviving Spouse*

- ☐ Notify post office for mail forwarding for surviving spouse.

- ☐ Clean living spaces.

- ☐ Pack up no-longer needed items.

- ☐ Clean out refrigerator and cabinets of perishables and outdated items.

- ☐ Safely dispose of medications. Information on safe disposal:
  - ☐ http://1.usa.gov/x8eLQj

- ☐ Do not move, sell, or give away items identified in the will that are to be distributed as part of the estate.

- ☐ Distribute these items to the legal beneficiary.

- ☐ Give away items to friends/family.

- ☐ Donate items to Goodwill or desired charity.

- ☐ Donate books to public or school libraries.

- ☐ Donate CDs to senior citizen homes or assisted-living residences.

- ☐ Sell items on eBay and/or Craigslist.

- ☐ Have an estate sale.

- ☐ Update automobile title and registration.

- ☐ Sell or donate car.

- ☐ Transfer car title to new owner.

- ☐ Cancel driver's license.

- ☐ Cancel voter registration.

- ☐ Sell or donate boats and other items at your state's Department of Motor Vehicles.

- ☐ Arrange long-term care for pets.

- ☐ Schedule yard upkeep.

- ☐ Schedule regular maid service for surviving spouse.

- ☐ Create a telephone listing of important numbers for surviving spouse.

- ☐ Update address book for spouse.

- ☐ Create regular allowance for surviving spouse.

- ☐ Insure continuation and payment of surviving spouse's life insurance, if policy exists.

- ☐ Insure continuation and of primary residence home insurance.

- ☐ Determine other needs of surviving spouse.

WRITING *the* EULOGY

A eulogy honors and commemorates life and provides an opportunity for the speaker to reminisce about personal details and positive circumstances surrounding the life of a loved one.

Eulogy Contents

The contents of a eulogy depend on the speaker or on the person who has directed you to give the eulogy. Keep in mind, the most successful and meaningful eulogies are written from the heart and delivered with compassion.

Eulogies may be humorous or serious, or be a combination of both. The best eulogies take the audience through a range of emotions and highlight the essence of the deceased.

Anecdotes and stories that show how loved the person was or how funny or quirky he/she was can lighten the mood. These stories can give funeral attendees a chance to recall positive memories of experiences that they had with the deceased. These stories also show how your loved one has made an impact on your and others' lives.

A well-written eulogy captures your loved one's personality and character. Feature his/her funny expressions, express core values, tell stories of humorous habits, talk about his/her illustrious job history, or show how the person was kind and giving. Most importantly, tell how you were inspired by your loved one's life.

You may want to share important milestones in his/her life, some unique aspect of his/her family history, or provide details about his/her perspective on life.

Structure and Approach

The structure and approach you choose is matter of style. The eulogy can be at its simplest the reading of a well-chosen poem or a condensed life history.

The presentation should be no longer than 10 minutes. If more than one person will be speaking, shorter is better. Provide your expectations on time limits to other speakers.

For all who plan to speak, whether it's one person or several, be prepared. This is an important responsibility and honor. If you need to ask family members about specific details, do so. They will be more than willing to help.

Preparation and Delivery

Use an outline or key words to guide your presentation. Reading a eulogy word for word may seem like the safe way to deliver the speech, but it's not the best way to honor the life of someone. And certainly not a comfortable situation for those listening to you read. Put some life into the presentation.

Writing a eulogy with a theme can enhance the cohesiveness of the presentation. Other ways to organize the information include the following: introduction, three main points, and conclusion. Some presenters opt for an audiovisual presentation and a spoken presentation. The most common is the eulogy in-person speech.

Delivering a eulogy is a rewarding and healing experience for both the speaker and those present. Speaking from the heart for this moment and delivering your personal thoughts, emotions, and stories are more important than a perfect presentation.

Speaking slowly with meaningful pauses and using an informal and conversational delivery in the conveyance of your deepest sympathies will ensure that your words and stories can touch the hearts of others and heal some of the sadness that they feel.

During the eulogy, you may have the tendency to become emotional. It's normal to cry and shed tears while you are presenting. Having tissues on hand is a good idea.

Don't Forget to Breathe

Remember to breathe deeply. If you start to cry, simply bow your head for a moment, then continue. People will understand. Just be strong and remember the reason you are standing before them.

Share your prepared remarks with another family member or the funeral director. If you are not able to continue the eulogy, they should be instructed to step in.

Most importantly, the eulogy should be about the celebration of someone's life and the mark that they made on the world.

1. A Sample Eulogy

For my mother's eulogy, I told a collection of related stories and provided details about how she defined her life. I embedded stories and humor. I cried, softly. I continued to speak while the tears streamed down my face. It was something that I couldn't control. I made people laugh. I made them cry more when I shared what she meant to me. I want to share with you what I delivered.

Margie B. Vincent's Eulogy - January 14, 2011

I am Margie's daughter, Donna. Thank you for coming today to share in and celebrate her life and her passing.

All of us today have a piece of my mother, Margie Vincent, inside of us. We carry what she gave. And she gave so much: laughter, loyalty, love, kindness and an intense spirituality.

My mother got on her knees every night to pray. I remember as a child running into her room to tell her something and stopping at the doorway when I saw her in prayer.

I knew not to disturb her. I knew she would be praying for me. She always prayed for me and for others. I am sure that those prayers have kept each of our families and us safe and sound.

She was a person who was so other-oriented and always selfless in her thoughts and actions. She was a giver. Of her time, her love, and of anything you said you wanted.

She would rather give something away and make someone happy than to keep something herself. She shared more than anyone I know. You almost had to be careful what you would say that you liked.

If you'd say, "That's a nice vase," or "That's a nice set of cards," you can be sure that it would be in your purse or suitcase before you left to go home.

The day that she fell and broke her hip, she continually said: "I'm O.K. I'm O.K." I remember that moment so well. Even in this moment of intense pain, she didn't want to burden anyone.

She never wanted to burden anyone. She always thought about others first.

When she broke her hip, as bad as that was, her 2.5 month stay with my family was a gift. Every night during that time, she had dinner with me, Victor, Alex and Gretchen.

I am blessed to have had the chance for my children to share this time with her. She shared her love, her stories, and her wisdom with all of us.

She disciplined my children and counseled my husband and me on the importance of raising children with values and with God.

Her view of life is something we all loved about her. She treasured her family, friends, fun, and God.

She always had a pot of coffee on and felt honored when friends stopped by for a visit. No one ever needed an appointment or even needed to call. Her door was always open to visitors and friends.

She could talk to you for hours and hours.

I remember when I first got married and my husband marveled how long I would talk. He would even ask, "What do you talk about for so many hours?"

Mama could always find something to talk about. I believe that she loved conversations more than she loved money, or anything for that matter.

She knew the importance of relationships and treasured every one that she had. How many people can say they have friends of 40 or 50 years? People came around Mama because she brought and gave happiness to everyone.

She was also woman whose heart was filled with fun. Her view of fun was like no other. She always played, was always ready to play. She loved to play cards. Rummy, Phase 10, Black Jack, and so many other cards games I can't even begin to remember them all.

And, there's one thing I am sure of...that she has won money playing cards from nearly everyone in this room.

Mama played with us when we were growing up. We were lucky to have a stay-at-home mother. She taught us a sense of gamesmanship and to be a good sport at everything. I remember when she would sit with us and play jacks. She would always win. It was nice to watch her graceful and quick hands pick up those metal jacks.

And, it wasn't just jacks.

She played first base on a mixed-league softball team until she was 40. The only reason she quit was because a ball thrown by the shortstop hit her in the face and broke her nose. It took a broken nose to take her out of the game.

For those of you who knew her well, she thrived on laughter. For me, I could come home at the times in my life when I needed to laugh, when I needed conversation. I could count on that from my mother. She could always help me to find the funny side of anything, no matter what. I cherished her view of life.

She had that rare gift to accept funny behavior and give you the confidence to keep on being funny or to find more funny stories to share. I would walk away feeling that I could really make people laugh.

One of the biggest laughing fests we had was when she travelled with me on a two-week trip around Europe. I was in England on a Rotary Scholarship and wanted to take a vacation before I came back to the United States.

She, my grandmother, my cousin and her grandmother met me in London, then we took a bus trip to 11 countries in Europe.

In Innsbruck, Austria, a tablespoon of bird poop landed on the top of her head. She yelled out her classic, "Now ain't that the shits?" and started laughing like a crazy women.

I started laughing, and we both ended up in the ladies room because we couldn't control other things if you know what I mean. People thought we were crazy. And, we were.

My mother had an awesome approach and attitude about life. She only went to the 8th grade, but she knew the importance of learning. She stimulated in all of us a love of learning. She would create games for us using the encyclopedia. And, when she didn't know something, she would always say, "Let's go look it up!" And we did.

She was never ashamed that she didn't have more education, though she often commented to me that she wish she had had the chance to go to school. It just wasn't in the cards for her. She devoted her life to her children and her family.

She always had expectations for and interest in our achievements. She was always eager to hear about what's next. And because she embedded in us a strong work ethic and a "you can do anything in life" attitude, she saw the fruits of her labor come back ten-fold.

I have her lessons, her stories, her love, and her laughter inside of me.

So many of us in this room do. They live on. We will carry them with us.

God has called her to heaven today. We must say good-bye. It's one of hardest things I've ever had to do in my adult life. You just don't want to say good-bye to your mother.

I am sure she's up there playing cards already.

Thank you for being here for her and for our family. God bless you.

EPILOGUE

I began the journey of writing this book about funerals and funeral planning to help others face death head on…to be ready. Through the process and accompanying research, I learned more about the possibilities and end-of-life options available to all of us. This also caused me to reflect on my own funeral and to think about my personal goals for when I die.

If I match my values and my way of thinking about the environment, I must package my death differently. I don't think traditional burial is right for me.

I want my last act on earth to have minimal environmental impact. My work in the environment and my concern for the impact we are having on this earth affect how I think and act. Why not how I die?

I am looking for a death that will be in harmony with my low-impact life. I support the values of greenspace preservation, carbon sequestration, and habitat creation.

Die and leave nothing to harm the earth. That's what I want. Allow me to be buried in a meadow or woodland glade right in the middle of a wildlife habitat. It's not wrong to think about a green funeral, stipulate your green funeral concerns in your will, and put in place environmentally conscious rituals.

I am drawn to the idea of a bamboo coffin (wider at the shoulders and tapers towards the feet) or a banana leaf casket (rectangular-shaped, same width from top to bottom) lined in cotton. These low impact and environmentally friendly alternatives use selectively harvested organic and sustainable materials, no glues or metal fasteners, and are free of formaldehyde, chemicals, pesticides, and other preservatives.

I saw an ad with the words "Bury Me Naturally." I have to admit that there's something romantic about being buried in a silk, cotton or woolen shroud instead of a cold metal casket that seems to slam shut in that last good-bye to life on earth. Kinkaraco.com, for example, offers a 100% natural and biodegradable shroud made of raw Dupioni silks and hand-woven wools that includes an exclusive herbal lining layer of aromatic herbs and fresh petals sewn between the fine netting and cotton batting. It's the one that I want.

While it is easy to follow traditions and to do what is expected, for many the traditional funeral with the embalmed body in a metal casket placed in a concrete vault may not be the right choice. Some of us will want to green the end of our life. Dying green isn't just for hippies or super-environmentalists.

Ecological funerals meet the needs of our generation...a generation that receives news of climate change and global warming on a daily basis and one that is more aware of the need for environmentally friendly ways of living and of dying.

I want an ecological funeral and burial. One that is simple, less wasteful of time, money, and natural resources. With the shortage of land, the cost of funerals, the environmental impact of cemeteries, now is the time to advocate for the concept.

Conventional death care practices have tremendous environmental impact. Each year tons of wood, steel, copper, bronze, reinforced concrete, and the millions of gallons of embalming fluid are buried in the over 22,500 cemeteries in the United States alone.

Natural burial grounds and green cemeteries represent more sustainable solutions. I believe that we will see a transition to more sustainable alternatives. In the last five years, the environmentally conscious are choosing green burials over traditional burial and cremation. Green burials allow the body to decompose naturally and do not pose future public health hazards.

Green can be associated with dying, and having a green or greener funeral comes down to an ethical, as well as a philosophical choice. We can reduce the environmental impact of our death.

The Green Burial Council defines green burial as "a way of caring for the death with minimal environmental impact that furthers legitimate ecological aims such as the conservation of natural resources, reduction of carbon emissions, protection of worker health, and the restoration and/or preservation of habitat." This kind of burial celebrates the life/death cycle and embraces the earth-to-earth philosophy.

At one cemetery in California where there are no headstones or caskets, survivors can locate their loved ones with a handheld GPS location finder.

Perhaps there's even a middle ground. All of us should think about ways we can make our funerals green.

Cremation may seem like a more sustainable, and certainly less expensive option, than a conventional burial, but environmental costs of cremation may be more than we bargained for. The estimated energy to cremate one body and a special coffin at temperatures as high as $2,100°F$ is about the amount of fuel required to drive nearly 5,000 miles.

The flames also expel cadmium and lead from pacemakers, and mercury from dental amalgams. It's been reported that vaporized dental amalgam accounts for 16% of the air-borne mercury pollution in the United Kingdom.

Alkaline hydrolysis is a new, greener alternative to cremation. The 3-hour bio-cremation process uses water, heat, pressure and potassium hydroxide to reduce the body to just bones, which are then processed into a fine white powder.

Ecological champions say this process uses less energy and produces less carbon dioxide and pollutants than cremation, but is not widely available in the United States as of this writing.

~~~

I believe that we need to be responsible for the material consequences of our decisions. Throughout any funeral planning process, ask questions. You have choices and options at all points of the funeral-planning continuum.

As for my funeral and burial and my final statement of my ecological values, I want to return to Mother Nature's embrace in the greenest way possible…a natural burial in my 100% biodegradable silk and wool shroud and to be laid to rest in a green meadow. Prairie Creek Conservation Cemetery in Gainesville, Florida, seems like that place in my dreams where I would like to be buried.

RESURCES *for a* GREENER FUNERAL

These links are provided for informational purposes only and not as an endorsement or a recommendation for use.

Natural or Conservation Burial
http://bit.ly/vnOcmI
http://bit.ly/greenerfuneral

Center for Natural Burial
http://bit.ly/uNbgEa

Green Burial Council
http://bit.ly/s9wWiF

Green Cemeteries
http://bit.ly/greencemeteries

Finding a Green Funeral Provider
http://bit.ly/rPzK3O

Natural Burial in the USA
http://bit.ly/tevPb0

Burial Shrouds
http://bit.ly/burialshrouds

Green Burial Wash
http://bit.ly/greenburialwash

Green Cremation Urns for Scattering, Earth Burial and Ocean or Lake Water Burial
http://bit.ly/rJZtsE

Fertig Funeral Home – Green Burial Option
http://bit.ly/rNfFvo

List of Green Casket Providers
http://bit.ly/thVo37

Eternal Reefs – Living Legacies
http://bit.ly/vr9vPC

Home and Family-Directed Funerals
http://bit.ly/vY3BLL

Home Funeral Directory
http://bit.ly/t5ZvBQ

Home Funeral Guide
http://bit.ly/uJLGVe

Burial at Sea
http://1.usa.gov/vZeaHJ
http://bit.ly/uVabIp

EPA Rules for Burial at Sea
http://1.usa.gov/sGaqyb

GREEN CEMETERIES

ALABAMA

Spring Hill Memorial Gardens
600 Pierce Rd.
Mobile, AL 36608
251-639-0962
http://bit.ly/scwl8q

ARIZONA

Sunwest Cemetery
12525 Northwest Grand Ave.
El Mirage, AZ 85335
623-974-2054
http://bit.ly/sqgBVW

CALIFORNIA

Forever Fernwood
301 Tennessee Valley Rd.
Mill Valley, CA 94941
415-383-7100
http://bit.ly/vzOWD6

Joshua Tree Memorial Park
60121 29 Palms Hwy.
Joshua Tree, CA 92252
760-366-9210
http://bit.ly/sswSve

Soquel Cemetery

550 Soquel San Jose Rd.

Soquel, CA

408-205-9994

http://bit.ly/vSJ4cm

Sunset Lawn

4701 Marysville Blvd.

Sacramento, CA 95838

916-922-5833

http://bit.ly/t04pJJ

sacramento@lifemarkgroup.com

COLORADO

Roselawn Cemetery

2718 E. Mulberry St.

Ft. Collins, CO 80524

970-221-6810

DISTRICT OF COLUMBIA

Historic Congressional Cemetery

1801 E St., SE

Washington, DC 20003

http://bit.ly/vNc9Lx

202-543-0539

FLORIDA

Glendale Nature Preserve

297 Railroad Ave.

Defuniak Springs, FL 32433

850-859-2141

http://bit.ly/tTpi9d

Green Meadows
At Brooksville Cemetery
1275 Olmes Rd.
Brooksville, FL 34601
352-636-5372
http://bit.ly/vC23xH

Prairie Creek Conservation Cemetery
7204 SE County Rd., #234
Gainesville, FL 32641
352-317-7307
http://bit.ly/rKm3XX

Eternal Rest Green Cemetery
2966 Belcher Rd.
Dunedin, FL 34698
727-733-2300
http://bit.ly/u01OpQ

GEORGIA

Honey Creek
2625 Hwy. 212, SW
Conyers, GA 30094
770-483-7535
http://bit.ly/swH2zP

Milton Fields Natural Burial Ground
1150 Birmingham Rd.
Milton, Georgia 30004
770-751-1445
http://bit.ly/s5sAaW
info@miltonfieldsgeorgia.com

ILLINOIS

Roselawn Memorial Park
924 South 6th St.
Springfield, IL 62703
217-525-1661
http://bit.ly/uCQXBs

Windridge Memorial Park And Nature Sanctuary
915 Crystal Lake Rd.
Cary, IL 60013
847-639-6502
http://bit.ly/tify35

INDIANA

Kessler Woods Washington Park North Cemetery
2702 Kessler Blvd. West Dr.
Indianapolis, IN 46228
317-259-1253
http://bit.ly/sn3jZX

KANSAS

Lincoln City Cemetery – Hall Funeral Home
111 E. Elm St.
Lincoln, KS 67455
785-524-4549

MAINE

Cedar Brook Memorial Park
175 Boothby Rd.
Limington, ME 04049
207-637-2085
http://bit.ly/vwnQ6A
a.green.cemetery@gmail.com

Rainbow's End
48 Mill Creek Rd.
Orrington, ME 04474
207-825-3843

MICHIGAN

Eagle Harbor Cemetery
Eagle Harbor Township Office
321 Centre St.
Eagle Harbor, MI 49950
906-289-4407

Marble Park Cemetery
520 W. Main St.
Milan, MI 48160
734-439-5660
www.marbleparkcemetery.com

Mt. Carmel Cemetery
138 Goddell St.
Wyandotte, MI 48192
734-285-1722
www.ourladyofmountcarmel.org

The Preserve at All Saints Cemetery
4401 Nelsey Rd.
Waterford MI 48329
800-989-9633
www.michigannaturalburial.com

Ridgeview Memorial Gardens
0-5151 8th Ave., SW
Grandville, MI 49418
616-249-8439
www.ridgeviewmemorialgardens.com

MISSOURI

Gates of Heaven Cemetery
255 Jackett Rd.
Seligman, MO 65745
417-341-1800

Green Acres Cemetery
4603 John Garry Dr., 10
Southhampton Village
Columbia, MO 65203
888-325-2653
www.mo-greenburial.com/services.html

NEW JERSEY

Maryrest Cemetery & Mausoleum
770 Darlington Ave.
Mahwah, NJ 07430
201-327-7011

Steelman Town Cemetery
327 Marshallville Rd.
Tuckahoe, NJ 08270
609-628-2297
www.steelmantowncemetery.com

Union Cemetery
(No Vaults)
195 Route 50
Mays Landing, NJ 08330
unioncemetery@aol.com

NEW MEXICO

Commonweal Conservancy
117 N. Guadalupe St., Suite "C"
Santa Fe, NM 87501
505-982-0071
www.commonwealconservancy.org

NEW YORK

Greensprings Natural Cemetery
293 Irish Hill Rd.
Newfield, NY 14867
607-564-7577
www.naturalburial.org

Sleepy Hollow Cemetery
540 North Broadway
Sleepy Hollow, NY 10591
914-631-0081
www.sleepyhollowcemetery.org

White Haven Memorial Park
210 Marsh Rd.
Pittsford (Rochester), NY 14534
585-586-5250
www.whitehavenmemorialpark.com

NORTH CAROLINA

Green Hills Cemetery
Hybrid Burial Ground
24 New Leicester Hwy.
Asheville, NC 28806
828-252-9831
www.greenhillscemeteryasheville.com

Pine Forest Memorial Gardens
Hybrid Burial Ground
770 Stadium Dr.
Wake Forest, NC 27587
919-556-6776
www.pineforestmemorial.com

OHIO

Foxfield Preserve
9877 Alabama Ave., SW
Wilmot, OH 44689
330-763-1331
www.foxfieldpreserve.org

OKLAHOMA

Green Haven Cemetery
P.O. Box 616
Stillwater, OK 74076
405-123-4567

OREGON

Estacada Cemetery District
P.O. Box 1390
Estacada, OR 97023
503-730-0142

Riverview Cemetery
0300 SW Taylors Ferry Rd.
Portland, OR 97219
503-246-4251
info@riverviewcemetery.org

Valley Memorial Park
3929 SE Tualatin Valley Hwy.
Hillsboro, OR 97123
503-648-5444
www.valleymemorialpark.com

PENNSYLVANIA

Oakwood Cemetery
Hybrid Burial Ground
600 N. Oakland Ave.
Sharon, PA 16146
724-346-4775

West Laurel Hill Cemetery
Hybrid Burial Ground
215 Belmont Ave.
Bala Cynwyd, PA 19004
610-664-1591
www.forever-care.com

SOUTH CAROLINA

Greenhaven Preserve
1701 Vanboklen Rd.
Eastover, SC 29044
803-403-9561
www.greenhavenpreserve.com

Ramsey Creek Preserve
390 Cobb Bridge Rd.
Westminster, SC 29693
864-647-7798
www.memorialecosystems.com

SOUTH DAKOTA

Mt. Pleasant Cemetery Association
Hybrid Burial Ground
2001 E. 12th St.
Sioux Falls, SD 57103
605-339-4760
www.mtpleasantsf.com

TENNESSEE

Grandview Cemetery
2304 Tuckaleechee Pike
Maryville, TN 37803
865-982-3730
www.smithmortuary.com

TEXAS

Eloise Woods Natural Burial Park
115 Northside Ln.
Cedar Creek, TX 78612
512-796-5240
www.eloisewoods.com

Our Lady Of The Rosary
330 Berry Ln.
Georgetown, TX 38626
512-863-8411
www.olotr.com

UTAH

Lakeview Cemetery
1640 E. Lakeview Dr.
Bountiful, UT 84010
801-298-1564
www.memorialutah.com

VIRGINIA

Duck Run Natural Cemetery
3173 Spotswood Trail
Harrisonburg, VA 22801
540-434-1359

WASHINGTON

Moles Greenacres Memorial Park
5700 Northwest Dr.
Ferndale, WA 98248
360-380-1784
www.molesfuneralhomes.com

White Eagle Memorial Preserve
401 Ekone St.
Goldendale, WA 98620
206-350-7353
www.naturalburialground.com

Woodlawn Cemetery
Hybrid Burial Ground
7509 Riverview Rd.
Snohomish, WA 98290
360-568-5560
www.woodlawncemeterysnohomish.com

WISCONSIN

**The Natural Path Sanctuary
At the Farley Center**
2299 Spring Rose Rd.
Verona, WI 53593
608-845-8724
262-524-3540
www.farleycenter.org

Prairie Home Cemetery
605 S. Prairie Ave.
Waukesha, WI 53186
262-524-3540
www.prairiehomecemetery.com

LIVING WILL *and* POWER *of* ATTORNEY RESOURCES

The information provided here is not a substitute for an attorney or a law firm. The sites listed here are provided for additional information and to familiarize you with the types of resources available. Your review of these resources can prepare you for conversations with an attorney and can be used to draw out your intentions. These sites provide access to templates that include similar questions that an attorney would ask for this type of transaction.

If you choose to use any legal form you find on the Internet, you should have it reviewed by a lawyer to ensure that it meets your specific legal needs and is valid in the state where you reside.

Each state has its own requirements for these kinds of transactions. Louisiana, for example, has unique estate laws: the principle of "forced heirship"—a provision of law that guarantees a child a share of his parents' estate with or without a will—is from the Napoleonic Code (CC1493) and does not appear on the books in any state.

Additionally, some forms may have outdated information, be based on outdated laws, be incomplete, have insufficient customization, not be flexible, or be the right tool for your particular tax issue (e.g., structuring trusts to reduce estate tax liability).

If you have additional legal questions or need expert assistance, you should contact a competent attorney licensed to practice in your state.

Inclusion in this list of resources implies no endorsement of the site, its tools and forms, or the services provided on the site. This list is for informational purposes only.

Living Will – Basic Information
http://bit.ly/uBHJlb

Caring Connections – What Are Advance Directives?
http://bit.ly/tRibwS

Preparing an Advance Directive – Forms and Instructions by State
http://aarp.us/tEhlyK

PrepareCase Online Legal Solutions
http://bit.ly/trRYIS

USLegal
http://bit.ly/scAvGA

FindLaw
http://bit.ly/sIJHlW

Legacy Writer
http://bit.ly/sR9fc1

Legalzoom.com
http://bit.ly/syEgCT

Sample Living Will
http://bit.ly/rvKpd5

LawDepot.com – Power of Attorney Form
http://bit.ly/ubqenH

Rocket Lawyer – The Easiest Way to Make It Legal
http://bit.ly/v3gMkj

Forms Tool
http://bit.ly/uggL5q

ADDITIONAL RESOURCES

These links are provided for informational purposes only and are not an endorsement or recommendation for use.

Organizing Your Papers
The 25 Documents You Need Before You Die
http://on.wsj.com/vUfxxX

Talking About What's Important to You
http://bit.ly/gowishcards

Estate Planning Information Center
http://bit.ly/uUplr4

Top Ten Estate Planning Techniques
http://bit.ly/u2xKt0

Estate Planning, Probate and Elder Law Information
http://bit.ly/s8RjJd
http://bit.ly/vxSnUg

Commission on Law and Aging
http://bit.ly/rR57Wl

Wills, Trusts, Powers of Attorney, American Bar Association
Estate Planning FAQ
http://bit.ly/vVq6HJ

Should You Have a Will?
http://bit.ly/t1r5d6

Cost-Effective Wills
http://aarp.us/uxoqLT

Ten Things You Should Know about Writing a Will
http://aarp.us/rpUPja

Why Is a Power of Attorney Important?
http://aarp.us/v06G8Y

Ethical Wills
http://bit.ly/ethicalwills

Organ Donation
http://1.usa.gov/suT6QB

United Network for Organ Sharing
http://bit.ly/organsharing

Register to Become a Donor
http://1.usa.gov/ug5MGi

Southeast Tissue Alliance
http://bit.ly/tissuealliance

Whole Body Donation to Science
http://bit.ly/sjkgWI

Whole Body Donation to Science (registration)
http://bit.ly/sGlW07

Body Donation Institutions
http://bit.ly/u4W0xk
http://bit.ly/uGqeJv

How Social Security Can Help You When A Family Member Dies
http://1.usa.gov/vvTSbt

Department of Veterans Affairs National Cemeteries
http://1.usa.gov/rrm72A

ADDITIONAL RESOURCES

List of State Veterans Cemeteries
http://1.usa.gov/tKg22v

Why Cremation?
http://bit.ly/uD8EbB
http://bit.ly/uWqX0m

Ash Scattering and Disposal
http://bit.ly/v3nxMG

Funeral Consumers Alliance
http://bit.ly/t8bExx

Coping with Grief and Loss
http://bit.ly/uo9AX9
http://bit.ly/u9zozS

A Guide for the Newly Widowed
http://aarp.us/tk0f3A
http://bit.ly/vefPM0

Six Characteristics of Helpful Ceremonies
http://bit.ly/umRYSB

Cultural and Religious Funeral Customs
http://bit.ly/vT5Wz6

Funeral Webcasting
http://bit.ly/uNl0Y4

Memorial Items
http://bit.ly/ui9c5I

notes

}

DONATIONS

DONATION TYPE	NAME AND ADDRESS	THANK YOU
		☐
		☐
		☐
		☐
		☐
		☐
		☐

DONATION TYPE	NAME AND ADDRESS	THANK YOU
		☐
		☐
		☐
		☐
		☐
		☐
		☐

OTHER WEB ACCOUNTS

Website and Login Information

Web Address:

Login Name:

Password:

Web Address:

Login Name:

Password:

Web Address:

Login Name:

Password:

Web Address:

Login Name:

Password:

Web Address:

Login Name:

Password:

Web Address:

Login Name:

Password:

Web Address:

Login Name:

Password:

Web Address:

Login Name:

Password:

Web Address:

Login Name:

Password:

TASKS *and* NOTES

- [ ] _____
  _____
- [ ] _____
  _____
- [ ] _____
  _____
- [ ] _____
  _____
- [ ] _____
  _____
- [ ] _____
  _____
- [ ] _____
  _____
- [ ] _____
  _____
- [ ] _____
  _____

- [ ] _____
  _____
- [ ] _____
  _____
- [ ] _____
  _____
- [ ] _____
  _____
- [ ] _____
  _____
- [ ] _____
  _____
- [ ] _____
  _____
- [ ] _____
  _____
- [ ] _____
  _____
- [ ] _____
  _____
- [ ] _____
  _____

BIO DATA

Full Name:

_____

Social Security #:

Address:

_____

City:

State/Zip/Country:

Date of Birth:

Place of Birth:

Date of Death:

Occupation:

Place of Work:

Address:

_____

_____

Marital Status:

Armed Forces Serial Number:

_____

Education: _____

_____

Siblings: _____

_____

_____

_____

_____

_____

_____

_____

Decedent's parents' names including middle initial:

Name of Father (first, middle, last): _____

_____

_____

_____

Name of Mother (first, maiden, last): _____

_____

_____

_____

OBITUARY INFORMATION

Full Legal Name: _____

Nickname: _____

Day and Date of Death: _____

Place of Death: _____

Residence (City and State): _____

Date of Birth: _____

Place of Birth: _____

List of Relatives:

Predeceased List: (deceased) _____

_____

_____

_____

_____

_____

_____

_____

_____

Survived by List: (still alive) _____

_____

_____

_____

_____

_____

_____

_____

_____

_____

_____

Workplace: _____

_____

_____

Retirement Information/Dates: _____

_____

_____

_____

Place of the Funeral: _____

_____

_____

Time of the Funeral: _____

Place of the Memorial Service: _____

_____

_____

Time of the Memorial Service: _____

Time of Burial/Graveside Services: _____

_____

_____

Burial Location: _____

_____

_____

Burial Officiant: _____

Names of Pallbearers:

_____

_____

_____

_____

_____

_____

_____

Memberships/Associations/Important Affiliations:

_____

_____

_____

_____

_____

_____

_____

_____

_____

Military Service:

_____

_____

_____

_____

_____

_____

_____

Special Interests and Achievements:

_____

_____

_____

_____

_____

_____

_____

_____

Donations to: (e.g., favorite charity, university, library, fraternal order, health organization, military association, community centers, dog shelter, etc.):

_____

_____

_____

_____

_____

_____

_____

_____

_____

_____

_____

_____

Flowers to: _____

_____

_____

_____

_____

_____

_____

_____

_____

_____

OBITUARY INFORMATION

Memorial Fund Established: _____

_____

_____

_____

_____

_____

_____

_____

Notes of Gratitude:

Other Special Information:

CALL LIST

☐ _____

_____

☐ _____

_____

☐ _____

_____

☐ _____

_____

☐ _____

_____

☐ _____

_____

☐ _____

_____

☐ _____

_____

☐ _____

_____

☐ _____

_____

☐ _____

_____

☐ _____

_____

☐ _____

_____

☐ _____

_____

☐ _____

_____

☐ _____

_____

☐ _____

_____

☐ _____

_____

☐ _____

_____

☐ _____

_____

IMPORTANT CONTACTS

Lawyer

_____

_____

_____

Accountant

_____

_____

_____

_____

Real Estate Agent

_____

_____

_____

_____

Insurance Agent

_____

_____

_____

_____

_____

Broker

_____

_____

_____

_____

_____

Banker

_____

_____

_____

_____

_____

Burial Insurance Provider

_____

_____

_____

_____

_____

Hairdresser

_____

_____

_____

_____

_____

Funeral Home

_____

_____

_____

_____

_____

Priest/Minister _____

_____

_____

_____

_____

_____

Cemetery _____

_____

_____

_____

_____

_____

Caterer _____

_____

_____

_____

_____

_____

Close Friends

_____

_____

_____

_____

_____

Neighbor

_____

_____

_____

_____

_____

LOCATION *of* IMPORTANT PAPERS

ITEM	LOCATION
Will	
Durable Health Care Power of Attorney	
Living Will	
Letter of Instruction	
Life Insurance Policies (personal)	

ITEM	LOCATION
Life Insurance Policies (from employer)	
Housing and Land Ownership	
Cemetery Plots	
Vehicles	
Stocks	
Savings Bonds	

ITEM	LOCATION
Partnership Agreements	
Business Operating Agreements	
Debts	
Marriage License	
Birth Certificate	
Divorce Papers/ Judgement	

ITEM	LOCATION
Child Support Payment Orders	
Qualified Domestic Relations Order	
Military Discharge Papers	
Tax Returns	

LIFE INSURANCE POLICIES

Carrier: _____

Agent: _____

Phone: _____

Address: _____

_____

Policy #: _____

Amount: _____

Carrier: _____

Agent: _____

Phone: _____

Address: _____

_____

Policy #: _____

Amount: _____

Carrier: _____

Agent: _____

Phone: _____

Address: _____

_____

Policy #: _____

Amount: _____

Carrier: _____

Agent: _____

Phone: _____

Address: _____

_____

Policy #: _____

Amount: _____

FOOD SCHEDULE/ DONATIONS

MEAL	WHAT?	WHO?
Date:		
Breakfast		
Lunch		
Dinner		
Date:		
Breakfast		
Lunch		
Dinner		

MEAL	WHAT?	WHO?
Date:		
Breakfast		
Lunch		
Dinner		

SAMPLE DURABLE POWER *of* ATTORNEY

This sample durable power of attorney was provided by the
National Hospice and Palliative Care Organization and should be
used for reference and information purposes only.

Each state has different requirements. This document, which is
used with permission from the organization, is a durable power of
attorney for the state of Maryland.

Additional information and forms for each state can be found at the
Caring Connections website: http://bit.ly/f5ohTf

MARYLAND
Advance Directive
Planning for Important Healthcare Decisions

Caring Connections
1731 King St, Suite 100, Alexandria, VA 22314
www.caringinfo.org
800/658-8898

Caring Connections, a program of the National Hospice and Palliative Care Organization (NHPCO), is a national consumer engagement initiative to improve care at the end of life.

It's About How You LIVE

It's About How You LIVE is a national community engagement campaign encouraging individuals to make informed decisions about end-of-life care and services. The campaign encourages people to:

Learn about options for end-of-life services and care
Implement plans to ensure wishes are honored
Voice decisions to family, friends and healthcare providers
Engage in personal or community efforts to improve end-of-life care

Note: The following is not a substitute for legal advice. While Caring Connections updates the following information and form to keep them up-to-date, changes in the underlying law can affect how the form will operate in the event you lose the ability to make decisions for yourself. If you have any questions about how the form will help ensure your wishes are carried out, or if your wishes do not seem to fit with the form, you may wish to talk to your health care provider or an attorney with experience in drafting advance directives.

Using these Materials

BEFORE YOU BEGIN
1. Check to be sure that you have the materials for each state in which you may receive healthcare.

2. These materials include:
   - Instructions for preparing your advance directive, please read all the instructions.
   - Your state-specific advance directive forms, which are the pages with the gray instruction bar on the left side.

ACTION STEPS
1. You may want to photocopy or print a second set of these forms before you start so you will have a clean copy if you need to start over.

2. When you begin to fill out the forms, refer to the gray instruction bars — they will guide you through the process.

3. Talk with your family, friends, and physicians about your advance directive. Be sure the person you appoint to make decisions on your behalf understands your wishes.

4. Once the form is completed and signed, photocopy the form and give it to the person you have appointed to make decisions on your behalf, your family, friends, health care providers and/or faith leaders so that the form is available in the event of an emergency.

5. You may also want to save a copy of your form in an online personal health records application, program, or service that allows you to share your medical documents with your physicians, family, and others who you want to take an active role in your advance care planning.

SAMPLE DURABLE POWER *of* ATTORNEY

2

INTRODUCTION TO YOUR MARYLAND ADVANCE DIRECTIVE

This packet contains two legal documents, the Maryland Advance Directive that protects your right to refuse medical treatment you do not want or to request treatment you do want in the event you lose the ability to make decisions yourself, and the Maryland "After My Death" form, a document that allows you to record your decisions regarding organ donation and the final disposition of your remains.

The Maryland Advance Directive is divided into three parts. You may fill out Part I, Part II, or both, depending on your advance planning needs. You must complete Part III.

Part I, Selection of Health Care Agent, lets you name someone (an agent) to make decisions about your health care. This part becomes effective either immediately, or when your doctor determines that you can no longer make or communicate your health care decisions, depending on how you fill out the form.

Part II includes your **Treatment Preferences**. This is your state's living will. It lets you state your wishes about health care in the event that you can no longer speak for yourself. Part II has specific choices laid out for you in the event you have a terminal condition, are in a persistent vegetative state (permanent unconsciousness), or develop an end-stage condition. Alternatively, you can provide your own instructions. In addition, the form allows you to choose whether your agent will have flexibility in implementing your decisions or carry out your instructions exactly as you set them out.

Part II becomes effective when your doctor determines that you can no longer make or communicate your health care decisions.

Part III contains the signature and witnessing provisions so that your document will be effective.

Following the Maryland Advance Directive is a form, called "After My Death," which allows you to record your organ donation and final remains disposition preferences.

The Maryland Advance Directive form does not expressly address mental illness. If you would like to make advance care plans regarding mental illness, you should talk to your physician and an attorney about a directive tailored to your needs. The Maryland Department of Mental Health and Hygiene provides an advance directive focused on mental-health issues on its webpage at http://www.dhmh.state.md.us/mha/forms.html

Note: This document will be legally binding only if the person completing it is either: (1) 18 years of age or older, or (2) if under the age of 18, is married or is the parent of a child.

INSTRUCTIONS COMPLETING YOUR MARYLAND ADVANCE DIRECTIVE

How do I make my Maryland Advance Directive legal?

You must sign and date your advance directive in the presence of two witnesses, who must also sign and date the document.

Your agent may not be a witness. In addition, at least one of your witnesses must be someone who will not knowingly inherit anything from your estate or otherwise knowingly benefit from your death.

Whom should I appoint as my agent?

Your agent is the person you appoint to make decisions about your health care if you become unable to make those decisions yourself. Your agent may be a family member or a close friend whom you trust to make serious decisions. The person you name as your agent should clearly understand your wishes and be willing to accept the responsibility of making health care decisions for you.

You can appoint a second person as your alternate agent. The alternate will step in if the first person you name as an agent is unable, unwilling, or unavailable to act for you.

You cannot appoint as your agent:
- An owner, operator, or employee of your treating health care facility
- The spouse, parent, child, or sibling of any of the above health care facility-affiliated individuals

However, you may appoint a person who would otherwise be barred from being your agent if that person is your guardian, spouse, domestic partner, adult child, parent, sibling, or other close relative or close friend who could be appointed as your surrogate in the event you do not appoint an agent.

Should I add personal instructions to my Appointment of Health Care Agent?

One of the strongest reasons for naming an agent is to have someone who can respond flexibly as your health care situation changes and deal with situations that you did not foresee. If you add instructions to this document it may help your agent carry out your wishes, but be careful that you do not unintentionally restrict your agent's power to act in your best interest. In any event, be sure to talk with your agent about your future medical care and describe what you consider to be an acceptable "quality of life."

What if I change my mind?

If you decide to cancel your Maryland Advance Directive, you may do so at any time by:
- issuing a signed and dated written or electronic revocation,
- destroying or defacing your document,
- orally informing your doctor of your revocation, or
- executing another Maryland Advance Directive.

You should notify your agent, physician, and anyone who has a photocopy of your advance directive that you have revoked it.

How do I make my "After My Death" form legal?

You must sign and date your "After My Death" form in the presence of two witnesses, who must also sign and date the document.

MARYLAND ADVANCE DIRECTIVE

Planning for Future Health Care Decisions

PRINT YOUR NAME AND YOUR DATE OF BIRTH

By: _____

(Print Name)

Date of Birth: _____

(Month/Day/Year)

Using this advance directive form to do health care planning is completely optional. Other forms are also valid in Maryland. No matter what form you use, talk to your family and others close to you about your wishes.

This form has two parts to state your wishes, and a third part for needed signatures. Part I of this form lets you answer this question: If you cannot (or do not want to) make your own health care decisions, who do you want to make them for you? The person you pick is called your health care agent. Make sure you talk to your health care agent (and any back-up agents) about this important role. Part II lets you write your preferences about efforts to extend your life in three situations: terminal condition, persistent vegetative state, and end-stage condition. In addition to your health care planning decisions, you can choose to become an organ donor after your death by filling out the form for that too.

You can fill out Parts I and II of this form, or only Part I, or only Part II. Use the form to reflect your wishes, then sign in front of two witnesses (Part III). If your wishes change, make a new advance directive.

Make sure you give a copy of the completed form to your health care agent, your doctor, and others who might need it. Keep a copy at home in a place where someone can get it if needed. Review what you have written periodically.

© 2005 National Hospice and Palliative Care Organization. 2011 Revised.

145

SAMPLE DURABLE POWER *of* ATTORNEY

PART I: SELECTION OF HEALTH CARE AGENT

PART I

A. Selection of Primary Agent

I select the following individual as my agent to make health care decisions for me:

Name:

PRINT THE NAME, ADDRESS, AND TELEPHONE NUMBER(S) OF YOUR PRIMARY AGENT

Address: _____

_____

Telephone Numbers:_____
(home and cell)

B. Selection of Back-up Agents

(Optional; form valid if left blank)

1. If my primary agent cannot be contacted in time or for any reason is unavailable or unable or unwilling to act as my agent, then I select the following person to act in this capacity:

PRINT THE NAME, ADDRESS, AND TELEPHONE NUMBER(S) OF YOUR FIRST BACK-UP AGENT

Name: _____

Address: _____

_____

Telephone Numbers: _____
(home and cell)

PRINT THE NAME, ADDRESS, AND TELEPHONE NUMBER(S) OF YOUR SECOND BACK-UP AGENT

2. If my primary agent and my first back-up agent cannot be contacted in time or for any reason are unavailable or unable or unwilling to act as my agent, then I select the following person to act in this capacity:

Name: _____

Address: _____

_____

Telephone Numbers: _____
(home and cell)

146

SAMPLE DURABLE POWER *of* ATTORNEY

7

C. Powers and Rights of Health Care Agent

I want my agent to have full power to make health care decisions for me, including the power to:

1. Consent or not consent to medical procedures and treatments which my doctors offer, including things that are intended to keep me alive, like ventilators and feeding tubes;

2. Decide who my doctor and other health care providers should be; and

3. Decide where I should be treated, including whether I should be in a hospital, nursing home, other medical care facility, or hospice program.

I also want my agent to:

1. Ride with me in an ambulance if ever I need to be rushed to the hospital; and

2. Be able to visit me if I am in a hospital or any other health care facility.

This advance directive does not make my agent responsible for any of the costs of my care.

This power is subject to the following conditions or limitations:

(Optional; form valid if left blank)

PRINT
INSTRUCTIONS
HERE ONLY IF YOU
WANT TO LIMIT
YOUR AGENT'S
POWERS

_____

_____

_____

_____

© 2005 National
Hospice and
Palliative Care
Organization.
2011 Revised.

147

SAMPLE DURABLE POWER *of* ATTORNEY

D. How My Agent Is To Decide Specific Issues

I trust my agent's judgment. My agent should look first to see if there is anything in Part II of this advance directive, if I have filled out Part II, that helps decide the issue. Then, my agent should think about the conversations we have had, my religious or other beliefs and values, my personality, and how I handled medical and other important issues in the past. If what I would decide is still unclear, then my agent is to make decisions for me that my agent believes are in my best interest. In doing so, my agent should consider the benefits, burdens, and risks of the choices presented by my doctors.

E. People My Agent Should Consult

(Optional; form valid if left blank)

In making important decisions on my behalf, I encourage my agent to consult with the following people. By filling this in, I do not intend to limit the number of people with whom my agent might want to consult or my agent's power to make these decisions.

Name(s) Telephone Number(s):

_____

_____

_____

_____

_____

_____

_____

148

SAMPLE DURABLE POWER of ATTORNEY

PRINT THE NAMES AND TELEPHONE NUMBERS OF ANYONE YOU WANT YOUR AGENT TO CONSULT WITH IN MAKING DECISIONS FOR YOU (OPTIONAL)

9

F. In Case of Pregnancy

(Optional, for women of child-bearing years only; form valid if left blank)

If I am pregnant, my agent shall follow these specific instructions:

_____

_____

_____

_____

_____

_____

_____

G. Access to My Health Information - Federal Privacy Law (HIPAA) Authorization

1. If, prior to the time the person selected as my agent has power to act under this document, my doctor wants to discuss with that person my capacity to make my own health care decisions, I authorize my doctor to disclose protected health information which relates to that issue.

2. Once my agent has full power to act under this document, my agent may request, receive, and review any information, oral or written, regarding my physical or mental health, including, but not limited to, medical and hospital records and other protected health information, and consent to disclosure of this information.

3. For all purposes related to this document, my agent is my personal representative under the Health Insurance Portability and Accountability Act (HIPAA). My agent may sign, as my personal representative, any release forms or other HIPAA-related materials.

PRINT ANY INSTRUCTIONS IN THE EVENT YOU ARE PREGNANT WHEN A DECISION MUST BE MADE

© 2005 National Hospice and Palliative Care Organization. 2011 Revised.

149

SAMPLE DURABLE POWER *of* ATTORNEY

10

H. Effectiveness of This Part

(Read both of these statements carefully. Then, initial one only.)

My agent's power is in effect:

_____ 1. Immediately after I sign this document, subject to my right to make any decision about my health care if I want and am able to.

INITIAL ONLY ONE

OR

_____ 2. Whenever I am not able to make informed decisions about my health care, either because the doctor in charge of my care (attending physician) decides that I have lost this ability temporarily, or my attending physician and a consulting doctor agree that I have lost this ability permanently.

If the only thing you want to do is select a health care agent, skip Part II, and go to Part III to sign and have the advance directive witnessed. If you also want to write your treatment preferences, use Part II. Also consider becoming an organ donor, using the separate "After my Death" form for that.

150

SAMPLE DURABLE POWER *of* ATTORNEY

PART II: TREATMENT PREFERENCES ("LIVING WILL")

A. Statement of Goals and Values

(Optional; form valid if left blank)

I want to say something about my goals and values, and especially what's most important to me during the last part of my life:

_____

_____

_____

_____

(attach additional pages if needed)

B. Preference in Case of Terminal Condition

(If you want to state your preference, initial one only. If you do not want to state a preference here, cross through the whole section.)

_____ 1. Keep me comfortable and allow natural death to occur. I do not want any medical interventions used to try to extend my life. I do not want to receive nutrition and fluids by tube or other medical means.

OR

_____ 2. Keep me comfortable and allow natural death to occur. I do not want medical interventions used to try to extend my life. If I am unable to take enough nourishment by mouth, however, I want to receive nutrition and fluids by tube or other medical means.

OR

_____ 3. Try to extend my life for as long as possible, using all available interventions that in reasonable medical judgment would prevent or delay my death. If I am unable to take enough nourishment by mouth, I want to receive nutrition and fluids by tube or other medical means.

PART II

USE THIS SPACE TO DISCUSS YOUR ADVANCE PLANNING GOALS AND VALUES

ATTACH ADDITIONAL PAGES IF NEEDED

INITIAL YOUR PREFERENCE IN THE EVENT YOU ARE IN A TERMINAL CONDITION

INITIAL ONLY ONE PREFERENCE

© 2005 National Hospice and Palliative Care Organization. 2011 Revised.

151

SAMPLE DURABLE POWER *of* ATTORNEY

C. Preference in Case of Persistent Vegetative State

(If you want to state your preference, initial one only. If you do not want to state a preference here, cross through the whole section.)

If my doctors certify that I am in a persistent vegetative state, that is, if I am not conscious and am not aware of myself or my environment or able to interact with others, and there is no reasonable expectation that I will ever regain consciousness:

_____ 1. Keep me comfortable and allow natural death to occur. I do not want any medical interventions used to try to extend my life. I do not want to receive nutrition and fluids by tube or other medical means.

OR

_____ 2. Keep me comfortable and allow natural death to occur. I do not want medical interventions used to try to extend my life. If I am unable to take enough nourishment by mouth, however, I want to receive nutrition and fluids by tube or other medical means.

OR

_____ 3. Try to extend my life for as long as possible, using all available interventions that in reasonable medical judgment would prevent or delay my death. If I am unable to take enough nourishment by mouth, I want to receive nutrition and fluids by tube or other medical means.

INITIAL YOUR PREFERENCE IN THE EVENT YOU ARE IN A PERSISTENT VEGETATIVE STATE

INITIAL ONLY ONE PREFERENCE

152

SAMPLE DURABLE POWER of ATTORNEY

D. Preference in Case of End-Stage Condition

(If you want to state your preference, initial one only. If you do not want to state a preference here, cross through the whole section.)

If my doctors certify that I am in an end-stage condition, that is, an incurable condition that will continue in its course until death and that has already resulted in loss of capacity and complete physical dependency:

INITIAL YOUR PREFERENCE IN THE EVENT YOU DEVELOP AN END-STAGE CONDITION

_____ 1. Keep me comfortable and allow natural death to occur. I do not want any medical interventions used to try to extend my life. I do not want to receive nutrition and fluids by tube or other medical means.

OR

INITIAL ONLY ONE PREFERENCE

_____ 2. Keep me comfortable and allow natural death to occur. I do not want medical interventions used to try to extend my life. If I am unable to take enough nourishment by mouth, however, I want to receive nutrition and fluids by tube or other medical means.

OR

_____ 3. Try to extend my life for as long as possible, using all available interventions that in reasonable medical judgment would prevent or delay my death. If I am unable to take enough nourishment by mouth, I want to receive nutrition and fluids by tube or other medical means.

153

SAMPLE DURABLE POWER *of* ATTORNEY

E. Additional Instructions:

ADD OTHER INSTRUCTIONS, IF ANY, REGARDING YOUR ADVANCE CARE PLANS

THESE INSTRUCTIONS CAN FURTHER ADDRESS YOUR HEALTH CARE PLANS, SUCH AS YOUR WISHES REGARDING HOSPICE TREATMENT, BUT CAN ALSO ADDRESS OTHER ADVANCE PLANNING ISSUES, SUCH AS YOUR BURIAL WISHES

ATTACH ADDITIONAL PAGES IF NEEDED

(You may add additional instructions, if any, here. This section may be useful to you if you have crossed through the sections above, or if your concerns are not otherwise addressed by this form.)

© 2005 National Hospice and Palliative Care Organization. 2011 Revised.

F. Pain Relief

No matter what my condition, give me the medicine or other treatment I need to relieve pain.

G. In Case of Pregnancy

(Optional, for women of child-bearing years only; form valid if left blank)

ADD INSTRUCTIONS HERE IF YOU WANT DIFFERENT TREATMENT IN THE EVENT YOU ARE PREGNANT

If I am pregnant, my decision concerning life-sustaining procedures shall be modified as follows:

_____

_____

_____

_____

_____

H. Effect of Stated Preferences

INITIAL ONLY ONE, DEPENDING ON HOW STRICTLY YOU WANT YOUR TREATMENT PREFERENCES FOLLOWED

(Read both of these statements carefully. Then, initial one only.)

_____ 1. I realize I cannot foresee everything that might happen after I can no longer decide for myself. My stated preferences are meant to guide whoever is making decisions on my behalf and my health care providers, but I authorize them to be flexible in applying these statements if they feel that doing so would be in my best interest.

OR

_____ 2. I realize I cannot foresee everything that might happen after I can no longer decide for myself. Still, I want whoever is making decisions on my behalf and my health care providers to follow my stated preferences exactly as written, even if they think that some alternative is better.

155

SAMPLE DURABLE POWER *of* ATTORNEY

16

PART III

PART III: SIGNATURE AND WITNESSES

By signing below as the Declarant, I indicate that I am emotionally and mentally competent to make this advance directive and that I understand its purpose and effect. I also understand that this document replaces any similar advance directive I may have completed before this date.

SIGN AND DATE
YOUR DOCUMENT

_____
(Signature of Declarant)   (Date)

The declarant signed or acknowledged signing this document in my presence and, based upon personal observation, appears to be emotionally and mentally competent to make this advance directive.

YOUR WITNESSES
MUST SIGN AND
DATE AND LIST
THEIR TELEPHONE
NUMBERS HERE

_____
(Signature of Witness)   (Date)

Telephone Number(s): _____

_____
(Signature of Witness)   (Date)

Telephone Number(s): _____

ONE WITNESS
MUST NOT
KNOWINGLY
INHERIT ANYTHING
FROM YOU OR
OTHERWISE
KNOWLINGLY
BENEFIT FROM
YOUR DEATH

(Note: Anyone selected as a health care agent in Part I may not be a witness. Also, at least one of the witnesses must be someone who will not knowingly inherit anything from the declarant or otherwise knowingly gain a financial benefit from the declarant's death. Maryland law does not require this document to be notarized.)

© 2005 National
Hospice and
Palliative Care
Organization.
2011 Revised.

156

SAMPLE DURABLE POWER of ATTORNEY

17

AFTER MY DEATH

PRINT YOUR NAME AND DATE OF BIRTH

(This form is optional. Fill out only what reflects your wishes.)

By: _____
(Print Name)

Date of Birth: _____
(Month/Day/Year)

PART I

PART I: ORGAN DONATION

(Initial the ones that you want.)

Upon my death I wish to donate:

INITIAL ONLY ONE

_____ Any needed organs, tissues, or eyes.
_____ Only the following organs, tissues, or eyes:

_____

_____

I authorize the use of my organs, tissues, or eyes:

_____ For transplantation
_____ For therapy
_____ For research
_____ For medical education
_____ For any purpose authorized by law

INITIAL ALL THAT APPLY

I understand that no vital organ, tissue, or eye may be removed for transplantation until after I have been pronounced dead under legal standards. This document is not intended to change anything about my health care while I am still alive. After death, I authorize any appropriate support measures to maintain the viability for transplantation of my organs, tissues, and eyes until organ, tissue, and eye recovery has been completed. I understand that my estate will not be charged for any costs related to this donation.

PART II

PART II: DONATION OF BODY

INITIAL HERE IF YOU WANT YOUR BODY DONATED FOR MEDICAL STUDY

_____ After any organ donation indicated in Part I, I wish my body to be donated for use in a medical study program.

157

PART III

PART III: DISPOSITION OF BODY AND FUNERAL ARRANGEMENTS

I want the following person to make decisions about the disposition of my body and my funeral arrangements:

(Either initial the first or fill in the second.)

INITIAL ONLY ONE

_____ The health care agent who I named in my advance directive.

OR

_____ This person:

PRINT NAME, ADDRESS, AND TELEPHONE NUMBER OF THE PERSON YOU WANT TO MAKE DECISIONS REGARDING DISPOSITION OF YOUR BODY

Name: _____

Address: _____

_____

_____

Telephone Numbers: _____
                              (home and cell)

If I have written my wishes below, they should be followed. If not, the person I have named should decide based on conversations we have had, my religious or other beliefs and values, my personality, and how I reacted to other peoples' funeral arrangements. My wishes about the disposition of my body and my funeral arrangements are:

PRINT ADDITIONAL INSTRUCTIONS HERE, IF ANY

_____

_____

_____

_____

158

SAMPLE DURABLE POWER of ATTORNEY

19

PART IV: SIGNATURE AND WITNESSES

PART IV	

By signing below, I indicate that I am emotionally and mentally competent to make this donation and that I understand the purpose and effect of this document.

SIGN AND DATE YOUR DOCUMENT HERE

_____
(Signature of Donor)   (Date)

The Donor signed or acknowledged signing this donation document in my presence and, based upon personal observation, appears to be emotionally and mentally competent to make this donation.

HERE YOUR WITNESSES SIGN AND DATE AND PRINT THEIR TELEPHONE NUMBERS HERE

_____
(Signature of Witness)   (Date)

Telephone Number(s) _____

_____
(Signature of Witness)   (Date)

Telephone Number(s) _____

Sample

Courtesy of Caring Connections
1731 King St, Suite 100, Alexandria, VA 22314
www.caringinfo.org, 800/658-8898

159

SAMPLE DURABLE POWER *of* ATTORNEY

You Have Filled Out Your Health Care Directive, Now What?

1. Your Maryland Advance Directive and "After my Death" form are important legal documents. Keep the original signed documents in a secure but accessible place. Do not put the original documents in a safe deposit box or any other security box that would keep others from having access to them.

2. Give photocopies of the signed originals to your agent and alternate agent, doctor(s), family, close friends, clergy, and anyone else who might become involved in your healthcare. If you enter a nursing home or hospital, have photocopies of your documents placed in your medical records.

3. Be sure to talk to your agent(s), doctor(s), clergy, family, and friends about your wishes concerning medical treatment. Discuss your wishes with them often, particularly if your medical condition changes.

4. You may also want to save a copy of your form in an online personal health records application, program, or service that allows you to share your medical documents with your physicians, family, and others who you want to take an active role in your advance care planning.

5. If you want to make changes to your documents after they have been signed and witnessed, you must complete a new document.

6. Remember, you can always revoke your Maryland documents.

7. Be aware that your Maryland documents will not be effective in the event of a medical emergency. Ambulance and hospital emergency department personnel are required to provide cardiopulmonary resuscitation (CPR) unless they are given a separate directive that states otherwise. These directives, called "emergency medical services/do not resuscitate orders" or "EMS/DNR orders," are designed for people whose poor health gives them little chance of benefiting from CPR. These directives instruct ambulance and hospital emergency personnel not to attempt CPR if your heart or breathing should stop.

   Currently not all states have laws authorizing these orders. We suggest you speak to your physician if you are interested in obtaining one. **Caring Connections does not distribute these forms.** To get information about a physician's order form that allows emergency medical personnel to provide comfort care instead of aggressive interventions, call the Maryland Institute for Emergency Medical Services Systems at (410) 706-4367. You can also download the Maryland EMS/DNR Order at: http://www.miemss.org

21

ABOUT *the* AUTHOR

Donna Vincent Roa is Managing Partner & Chief Strategist for Vincent Roa Group LLC, a Maryland-based firm specializing in communication to improve the earth and its people™ − science, environment, sustainability, water, energy, technology, and public health communication.

An IABC-accredited business communicator, Donna is a business process expert who builds best-in-class communication portfolios for government agencies, corporate clients and international organizations.

Previously, she was Public Affairs Director and Director of Science Communication at the US Environmental Protection Agency. A former United Nations senior communication officer and water sector communication consultant for the World Bank and UNICEF, she was the keynote speaker at the first class of graduating social marketers in Cajamarca, Peru. She was also one of ten US Treasury Department-designated researchers to conduct research to support the first redesign of the $100 bill.

She is past president of the largest US chapter of the International Association of Business Communicators, has a Ph.D. in Communication from the University of Southern Mississippi, was a Rotary Scholar, and is a former Environment Commissioner for the City of Rockville.

Early in her career, she wrote obituary notices for the Beaumont Enterprise newspaper's Lake Charles, Louisiana Bureau.

She lives in Rockville, MD, with her husband, Victor, her children, Alex and Gretchen, and a rescue Chihuahua Shih Tzu, named Max.

Thank you for purchasing
The Ultimate To Do List When Your Loved One Dies
Before & After the Funeral

I welcome your feedback and comments about additional to do
items that should be included in subsequent editions of this book.

Your suggestions are appreciated and will play a part
in ensuring that readers are fully prepared
for before, during and after a loved one's funeral.

Please write to me at donna@funeraltodolist.com

I would like to hear your story
about how you used this planning tool.
I look forward to hearing from you.

Donna Vincent Roa

To order additional copies of this book or
to give copies to your friends and relatives,
visit Amazon.com and search:
The Ultimate To Do List When Your Loved One Dies
Before & After the Funeral